PROSECCO
MADE ME DO IT

PROSECCO MADE ME DO IT

60 SERIOUSLY SPARKLING COCKTAILS

AMY ZAVATTO

ILLUSTRATED BY RUBY TAYLOR

Andrews McMeel
PUBLISHING®

Andrews McMeel Publishing
a division of Andrews McMeel Universal
1130 Walnut Street, Kansas City, Missouri 64106

www.andrewsmcmeel.com

18 19 20 21 22 HPL 10 9 8 7 6 5 4 3 2

ISBN: 978-1-4494-9254-0

Library of Congress Control Number: 2017955430

ATTENTION: SCHOOLS AND BUSINESSES

Andrews McMeel books are available at quantity discounts
with bulk purchase for educational, business, or sales
promotional use. For information, please e-mail the Andrews
McMeel Publishing Special Sales Department:
specialsales@amuniversal.com.

CONTENTS

INTRODUCTION

The year is 1868. Louisa May Alcott's classic *Little Women* is first published. Australia ends its era as a penal colony for England. London installs the world's first traffic light. The first cro-magnon human remains are unearthed by French geologist Louis Lartet. And Antonio Carpané produces the very first bottle of sparkling Prosecco, gleaned from the breezy hills of Conegliano and Valdobbiadene in northern Italy.

Carpané could only have dreamed that, by the beginning of the 21st century, his fizzy, frothy experiment would become the most toasted of toastables the world over. And why not? Affordable Prosecco makes bubbles accessible. For years, sparkling wine was relegated to the special occasion—the wedding toast, the birth, the big job promotion, the holidays, but… what about all those other days during the year when a glass of something sparkly performs the happy miracle of putting a smile on your face? Prosecco whets the appetite, enlivens the senses with its beautiful, fruity aromatics, and makes a spectacular date at the dinner table.

From the traditional Bellini (see page 27) to the sophisticated Ship to Shore (see page 56), Prosecco adds lift and life. When paired with anything from juices to fortified aperitifs, it can be an easy two-ingredient tipple that you can whip up in seconds. When combined in a multi-ingredient cocktail, it elevates flavors and aromatics with its freshness and zippy bubbles. Like mustard, butter, and milk, it really should be in your refrigerator at all times.

Prosecco Made Me Do It is going to get you into that frame of mind ("Oh, a snowstorm's coming? Better get Prosecco!"). These sixty cocktails—from the easy-peasy and riffs on classics to entirely new-to-this-world creations—will not only become entertaining staples for your home bar, but if I have my way, they'll inspire you to come up with your own variations with this most charming of Italian sparkling wines, too. Let the Champagne drinkers hoard their bottles for a moment that never comes. Prosecco drinkers have more fun.

COSA È PROSECCO?

"What is Prosecco?"

I used to get this question a lot. Along with:
"It's Champagne, right?"
"It's sweet, right?"
"It's just cheap stuff, right?"

Then, it seems, the world at large had an "Ah-ha!" moment, and Prosecco was everywhere. A glass of Prosecco before dinner? Well, of course! A low-alcohol spritz to whet your whistle when out for drinks with friends? Absolutely! Wine lists and cocktail menus began to burst with options for the Italian fizzy stuff. And yet… the "What is Prosecco?" question lingers. It's popular! It's fun! It's Italian! What else do you need to know? It's all the same, right? Like anything, if it's worth the pleasure it provides when it passes your lips, it's worth learning a little bit about because, inevitably, those little bubbles of knowledge will help you make great choices—and, therefore, drink really well. Is Prosecco inexpensive? In comparison to high-end Champagne (which, by the way, can only be called that if it's made in the Champagne region using traditional methods), yes. But whether you're spending a little or a lot, you should know what you're getting. And that's what we're going to dive into here. What is Prosecco? Glad you asked…

PLACE OF POP

Prosecco is the name of the DOC (*denominazione di origine controllata*)—a regional designation which, when you see it on a wine label, is a way of assuring you that the product you are buying is made from certain ingredients in a particular place and in a certain way. It's a thumbs-up for hitting basic standards of quality. Groovy, right?

In the case of Prosecco, that place in question is about as northeast as you can go, reaching across the regions of Veneto to Friuli Venezia Giulia near the Adriatic Sea, and rimmed to the north by the Dolomite Mountains and the eastern rim of the Alps. Most wines from this broad area are designated as DOC on the label, but there are also three other special designations within it that speak to an even higher guaranteed level of quality and site specificity.

The first two are Treviso and Trieste. If you see either of those places listed on the label of your DOC-level Prosecco, that means the grapes and production happened within those specific areas.

There is a third zone, however, that the Italian government gave an even more special designation: the Conegliano Valdobbiadene DOCG (*denominazione di origine controllata e garantita*). That G? That means, along with all the other assurances like specific region and grape, the government is *guaranteeing* the actual quality of what you're about to drink. That's pretty cool!

Another one of those DOC standards is the grape or grapes that can be used: Glera grapes, which, for a while, were also called Prosecco. (So if you thought Prosecco was the actual name of the grape, don't feel bad.) All wines labeled as Prosecco must be made up of 85% of this Italian white grape variety, which is more often than not rife with beautiful orchard fruit notes. What's the other 15%? About five or so other indigenous white varieties (if you really want to know: Glera Tonda, Glera Lunga, Glera Verdiso, Glera Perera, and Glera Bianchetta Trevigiana), and, since the 1960s, four international grape varieties: Chardonnay, Pinot Grigio, Pinot Bianco, and Pinot Nero (or Noir, as you may know it better).

There are three ways the DOC permits Prosecco producers to make their bubbly, but by and large what you buy from your favorite local wine shop or grocery store is in the spumante style, which is super bubbly (there's also frizzante, with its more gentle bubbles, and a completely non-bubbly version, tranquilo).

THE DL ON THE DOCG

It's worth taking a closer look at Conegliano Valdobbiadene, as it is a concentrated, unique little spot. I know—it's super hard to say, so let's begin with a little phonetic pronunciation lesson: cone-ell-yanno. Not so hard, right? Next up: val-doe-be-ah-den-ay. That one's a little

trickier. But if you practice a few times, it'll start to roll around your tongue and out of your mouth like you're a real Italian. And, you know, who doesn't want to sound like a real Italian? I sure do.

Conegliano Valdobbiadene is a special place. It's home to the birthplace of Prosecco wine, where the oldest vines dwell on dizzyingly steep south-facing slopes, and only the gentle human hand can carefully pick the fruit. Here, the vines are warmed by the sun and cooled by the breezes off the Adriatic Sea, and sit in diverse plots of land that make for beautifully nuanced sparkling wines. Grapes have likely been grown here for thousands of years, but it's the late 20th century where things start getting really exciting for Prosecco.

In 1962, eleven local guys got together and said, you know, this place is pretty special! They formed the *Consorzio di Tutela del Prosecco di Conegliano e Valdobbiadene*. By 1969, the Italian government came around to agreeing (things take time in Italy—long lunches and all) and recognized the area as part of its special DOC system of quality.

But all along, Prosecco had been slowly but surely becoming more popular, thanks in part to Giuseppe Cipriani. Cipriani opened the famed Harry's Bar near the Piazza San Marco in Venice in 1931. It was here that he created a cocktail that not only outlasted his own life, but perhaps will still be poured long after the sea claims Venice for its own: the Bellini (see page 27). The irresistible mix of fresh white peach purée and Prosecco was a hit with both aristocrats and American soldiers stationed in Italy. They brought the drink to the US and, by the late 1960s, Prosecco began to appear in America; it had already crossed borders into other parts of Europe. Demand increased, and thus did production.

Fast forward to the aughts, and Glera-growing and Prosecco-making had spread far beyond the Congeliano-Valdobbiadene (C-V) borders into two full-on regions, nine provinces, and 556 villages. Prosecco, you see, is prolific. Grapes were being planted in the valleys, where they grew fast and loose and harvesting could be done with quick-grabbing machines, allowing more, more, more Prosecco to fill glasses the world over. The problem with that: it diluted the quality. How could you tell the difference between a hand-harvested complex Prosecco from the C-V hills and a fast and loose fandango, machine-harvested in the valley?

Up until the turn of the 20th century, the bubbles in Prosecco (and Champagne) were happening in the bottle via something called secondary fermentation. Fermentation is, simply, how alcohol happens: Yeast (which exists naturally, or can be added) eats sugar (which, voila! is in grapes) and you get alcohol. You get bubbles when a second fermentation happens within a small space, like a bottle. This was happening with Prosecco, but not with totally reliable results. Some bottles were more sparkly than others. Some were still wines. And some bottles even exploded. Yikes.

In 1895, a brilliant man named Federico Martinotti figured out how to make a more reliable bubbly product with the region's beloved Glera grapes. If that second fermentation could happen in large, pressurized wooden tanks, it could be better controlled. But it still wasn't totally reliable. Another smart person named Eugene Charmat came along a few years later, tinkered with Martinotti's technique, and invented a new tank in a more reliable material (stainless steel), that seemed pretty foolproof. And thus, the Charmat Method, by which nearly all Prosecco is produced, was born. Ta-da!

About 90 million bottles a year come from the DOCG zone, which is about 30 kilometers at its widest with around 7,000 hectares planted. So, that's about one case of Prosecco per year for every person living in Amsterdam or Hong Kong. Lucky them! But compare that to 420 million bottles coming out of the greater DOC area and about 20,000 hectares, and you start to get the picture. This is why in 2009 the government awarded C-V the special status of DOCG. When you pick up a bottle, this will be clearly stated on the label, along with the word "superiore," just for that extra-special emphasis. And for what it's worth, just outside of the western tip of Conegliano Valdobbiadene is a little (just shy of 200 hectares) spot called Asolo, which is another separate Prosecco DOCG adhering to the same parameters and standards of quality that C-V does. But within C-V, things actually get even more wine-geeky, so let's break it down...

Conegliano Valdobbiadene Prosecco Superiore

The oldest Prosecco producing spot, this DOCG was born (or, well, reborn) in 2009 to set its particularity apart from the rest of the Prosecco wines.

Rive

A super-special sub-zone designation, not unlike the villages of Burgundy. There are currently forty-three in total. If you see this word along with Conegliano Valdobbiadene Prosecco Superiore, it means the grapes come only from the rive named on the label. The other cool thing about that: It positions you a little deeper into the region, letting you know if the grapes in your juice are from the more dense soils of Conegliano, which tend to give you a little more richness in texture, or the shallow, rocky soils of Valdobbiadene, rife with marine-deposits. Wines from here tend to have more prominent floral and minerally notes and, call me crazy, but a little bit of that seaside salinity, too.

Cartizze

Let's just call this Prosecco Oz. It's a single little 107-hectare area within Valdobbiadene in the western reaches of the DOCG.

SWEET (AND NOT-SO-SWEET) SENSATIONS

As you learned above, all Prosecco is not created equal. So it's kind of funny how it got a rep for being sweet. Some are, sure, but certainly not all. How can you know? That's easy. Regardless of where your Prosecco came from within the region (or the region within the region within the region!), every bottle has a wonderful, simple clue. If your bottle says:

Extra Brut

This designation is pretty new (made official as of 2017, although certainly wines had been made in the past at this level of dryness), and means there are between 0 and 6 grams of sugar in the final product. If you like your sparkly dry like a cracker, this is for you.

Brut

This used to be the catch-all for extra brut, too, but now means you're at a dry 6–12 grams of sugar. Nice and dry.

Extra Dry

At 12–17 grams of sugar, this might seem a little confusing. Shouldn't "extra dry" mean… extra dry? Maybe, but it doesn't—it means the Prosecco in question has a nice easy-going bit of sweetness to it, but isn't cloying or over-the-top. When you're working with cocktails in which you want to play up the fruity essence in the drink, this is where you want to go.

Dry

At 17–32 grams of sugar, this not-so-dry sparkling is in the dessert zone. And if you don't have any simple syrup or bar sugar on hand, it can be great to play around with if you need just that little bit of extra sweetness to balance out other more savory or sour notes.

You'll notice in the recipes that I steer you toward one or another of these sweetness levels. That's worth paying attention to. Like any cocktail ingredient, you should consider what it brings to the final result. Some more juniper-heavy, herbaceous gins, for instance, make for an excellent Martini, while other more citrus-forward versions are key to a refreshing gin and tonic. Opt for one sweet vermouth or another, and your Manhattan takes on a whole new dimension. Same with Prosecco.

TOP TIPS

You now know how Prosecco came to be. You know where it's from and the nuances of the region and can walk into any wine store and pick like a pro! But before we jump into all the fun that's to come, let's go over a few basics to help set your Prosecco-cocktail concocting on a good path.

HOW TO OPEN A BOTTLE
Put that saber away, and for the love of Pete, DO NOT ever launch a cork into the atmosphere. The former is for the pros and the latter is just a silly, dangerous thing to do, no matter how fun it might seem. When you hit your best friend in the eye with a cork powered by 2.5 bars of pressure, I guarantee they will not be happy with you.

So do this instead:
1. Set the bottle on a solid surface, like a worktop.
2. Grab a tea towel or kitchen towel.
3. Place the towel over the top of the bottle.
4. Grab the base of the bottle securely with one hand, and put the other hand over the top of the towel-covered cork section.
5. Gently twist until the cork is released.

That's it. I swear, it's really easy. You won't lose tons of overflowing delicious Prosecco and no one gets hurt. No better way to get the party started right.

STORING YOUR WINE
Like any wine, store your Prosecco in a cool, dark, mildly humid place (like a basement, if you have one) on its side until you're ready to chill it and use it. Do not store it or any other wine for the long term in the refrigerator—the opening and closing of the door makes for lots of up and down in temperature and its just too dry of an atmosphere for the long haul with any wine. Definitely do not store your bottles

on top of the refrigerator, or any high-up area—heat rises! Heat is the enemy of wine, and definitely the arch rival of bubbles.

When ready to use your Prosecco, pop it in the refrigerator a few hours or up to a day or so beforehand.

It might sound bananas, but if you don't manage to finish an opened bottle (blasphemous!), use a simple Champagne stopper—these have a rubber seal that you press into the lip of the bottle and two side wings that fasten onto the rim. They're inexpensive, easy to find, and you can use them for beer and sparkling cider, too.

INGREDIENT CARE
Aside from spirits, cocktails require other ingredients, like fruits, herbs, and sweeteners like syrups.

When it comes to fruit, the number one rule: Always wash it! By wash, I mean rinse thoroughly with cool water. That goes for citrus, especially if you're using the zest as a garnish. With raspberries and blackberries, only gently rinse what you need—washing all of them at once and putting back the brunt that isn't going to go in your cocktail will lead to moldy fruit. All those little bumps and nooks and crannies hold the moisture and, thus, start to rot faster when wet. Blueberries and strawberries are an exception, but you should let them dry off on a towel before putting them back in your refrigerator.

As for herbs, gently rinse and pat dry. Store any extra like flowers with the stems in a container of water, or dampen a paper towel, wrap them up, and store in the crisper of your refrigerator.

SYRUPS

Many cocktails in this book require a touch of simple syrup. I prefer using this to superfine sugar or any granulated sugar, no matter how fine, because it's already dissolved and easier to mix. Make a batch ahead of time and store it in your refrigerator. The variations you can make on this are only limited by your imagination and ingredients, but here are the recipes contained in this book for your reference.

SIMPLE SYRUP
The basic recipe tells you a lot about the name: it's simple! The method is as follows:
1 part sugar to 1 part water.

Combine the sugar and water in a small saucepan over medium heat and gently stir until the sugar dissolves. Let cool, then store in an airtight container for up to 2 weeks.

MINT SIMPLE SYRUP
1 cup granulated white sugar
1 cup water
¼ cup fresh mint leaves, washed

Drop the mint into a small saucepan and gently muddle to release the oils. Add the sugar and water and cook over medium heat. Gently stir until the sugar dissolves and the aroma of the mint is prominent. Let cool, then store in an airtight container for up to 2 weeks.

VARIATIONS
Basil Simple Syrup—make as above but use basil instead of mint.
Rosemary Simple Syrup—make as above but use 3–4 fresh rosemary sprigs instead of mint.

Cinnamon Simple Syrup—combine 3 cinnamon sticks in the saucepan with the sugar and water and continue as before.
Honey Syrup—combine 1 cup honey with the water in a saucepan and continue as before.
Honey-Basil Syrup—combine 1 cup honey and ¼ cup fresh basil leaves with the water and continue as before.
Ginger Simple Syrup—cook the sugar and water as before and add a 10-inch (4-ounce) piece of ginger, peeled and very thinly sliced. Bring to a simmer, remove from the heat, and let steep for 30 minutes. Pour through a fine-mesh sieve into an airtight container.

CONCORD GRAPE SYRUP

The sweetness inherent in grapes means no sugar need apply. Simply take 2 cups rinsed Concord grapes (although any red or black grapes will do) and put them in a small saucepan. Cook over medium heat, stirring, until the grape skins begin to break, and the juice and flesh spill out into the pan. Cook down for about 5 minutes. Cool and press through a fine mesh sieve, discarding the extra pulp, skins and stems. Store in an airtight container for up to 2 weeks.

GRENADINE

Sure, you can buy it, but it won't taste half as good (and will likely have high-fructose corn syrup in the mix—yuck).

1 cup unsweetened pomegranate juice
1 cup granulated white sugar
1 teaspoon rose water

Combine the pomegranate juice, water, and rose water in a small saucepan over medium heat and gently stir until the sugar dissolves. Let cool, then store in an airtight container for up to 2 weeks.

PURÉES

There is no Bellini without peach purée. But, as a matter of fact, purées in general are a great cocktail ingredient, and specifically make a delicious dance partner for fruit-centric Prosecco. To keep the fruit from oxidizing, add a little lemon juice into the mix to help hold the color of the pretty fruit and keep it fresher longer.

WHITE PEACH PURÉE

2 cups ripe white peaches, washed and cut into
    quarters, pits discarded
1 fluid ounce freshly squeezed lemon juice
1½ fluid ounces Simple Syrup (page 16)

Purée all the ingredients in a blender or food processor until very smooth. Freeze or store in the refrigerator in an airtight container for up to a week.

VARIATIONS

Really anything goes in terms of fruits, so try using your favorite and experiment. Here are a few used in the book:
Strawberry Purée—make as above but use 2 cups washed, hulled, and halved strawberries, ¾ fluid ounce freshly squeezed lemon juice, and 1 fluid ounce Simple Syrup (page 16).
Spiced Pear Purée—make as above but use 2 cups ripe Bosc pears, washed and quartered, 1 fluid ounce freshly squeezed lemon juice, and 1½ fluid ounces Cinnamon Simple Syrup (page 17). To make this extra spicy, add a little star anise into the pan when you're making your Cinnamon Simple Syrup.
Watermelon Purée—make as above but use 2 cups cubed watermelon, ½ fluid ounce freshly squeezed lemon or lime juice, and 1 fluid ounce Simple Syrup (page 16).

ICE-CAPADES!

Ice is important in cocktails. Some bartenders might even tell you it's the most important ingredient. If your ice is old and smelly (yes, I'm talking to you, person who hasn't cleaned out the freezer in a really, really, really long time), your drink will reflect that nastiness. At the very least, make sure your ice is the product of a good environment.

Ice adds cold, obviously. But ice also adds the very important component of dilution. When it comes to punches, you do not want to add a pile of ice cubes—they will melt faster than you can pop your Prosecco, and ruin a perfectly good mass-scale drink. Instead, make an ice ring or ice block.

It's simple to do: Fill a clean bundt pan or large plastic storage container with water. Put it in your freezer a good 24 hours prior to your party.

To release the ice, run under cold (not hot!) water for a minute and then gently shake out into your punch bowl. That's it. It will dissolve much more slowly—and look pretty cool, too.

Up the ante by taking the garnish suggestions in the punch recipes starting on page 130 and drop them into the water of your ice ring before freezing. Voila—floating garnishes suspended in animation!

THE RECIPES

VENETIAN SPRITZ

(Makes 1)

The first time I had this refreshing, super-easy aperitif was not, as the name might imply, in Venice. It was in Red Hook, Brooklyn, one of the earlier settlements in New York City's history as an American Revolution point of defense and, eventually, a bustling port. The bar where the Venetian Spritz first passed my lips is called Fort Defiance, named for the stalwart spot that defended the area during the Battle of Long Island. But there was no battle when I sipped this lovely pre-dinner quencher. Aperol is a bitter Italian liqueur, lower in alcohol and a little sweeter than its similarly red-hued cousin, Campari. For that reason, it makes a lovely complement to Prosecco's typical orchard fruitiness. A brut-style balances the Aperol nicely. The olive? I was dubious, too, the first time I had this cocktail. But there was something about the sweet and sour that appealed to my cocktail-subversive side. If you are not so keen, feel free to simply sip this as-is, or with an orange slice.

Ingredients
1½ fluid ounces Aperol
3 fluid ounces brut-style Prosecco
Splash of club soda
1 Cerignola olive, red or green—your choice (optional)

Instructions
Fill a double rocks glass with ice. Pour in the Aperol followed by the Prosecco. Give it a little stir. Top up with a splash of club soda and garnish with a Cerignola olive.

PROSECCO SABA

(Makes 1)

The island of Sardinia sits off the west coast of Italy, its west and southern borders facing the Mediterranean Sea, the Tyrrhenian Sea to the east, and the Strait of Bonifacio separating its northern shores from Corsica. As it goes on islands, Sardinia maintains many unique particularities, like its language, Sardo—a mix of Latin, Arabic, Spanish, and Catalan—which tells you a lot about what a coveted spot Sardinia was before Italy claimed it for its own. Saba is one of the island's many unique little treasures. This sweet-tart, silky condiment is the product of cooked-down grape must (that is, the leftover juice, skins, pits, and stems after crushing). An extra dry-style Prosecco plays up the saba and makes a great aperitif.

Ingredients
¼ fluid ounce Saba
3 fluid ounces extra dry-style Prosecco

Instructions
Drizzle the Saba into a tulip glass, then slowly top with the Prosecco. Give it a little stir and serve.

BELLINI (TRADITIONAL)

(Makes 1)

One of the great things about Prosecco as a cocktail ingredient is that your choice of two-ingredient, ridiculously-easy-to-whip-up concoctions are nearly endless—as are the variations on what is perhaps the most famous of two-ingredient Prosecco cocktails: the Bellini. Famously invented by the owner of Harry's Bar in Venice, Giuseppe Cipriani, the drink originally calls for white peaches, but if all you have are beautiful, ripe yellow peaches, that's just fine, too.

Ingredients
1 fluid ounce White Peach Purée (page 18)
3 fluid ounces brut-style Prosecco

Instructions
Pour the White Peach Purée into a flute. Top with the Prosecco, give it a little stir, and serve.

TROPICAL BELLINI

(Makes 1)

It's Saturday night. The air is balmy, but a beautiful breeze drifts through your window. If you call up some fado on your iPod and close your eyes, you can almost conjure up that vacation you took last year to the beaches of Brazil. Better yet, make one of these. Passion fruit are native to South America. Use the instructions on page 18 to make your own purée, or else feel perfectly free to seek out a high-quality bottled version at your local gourmet food store (as straining out the edible seeds through a sieve from the fresh version might put a damper on your nice daydream).

Ingredients
1 fluid ounce passion fruit purée
3 fluid ounces brut-style Prosecco

Instructions
Pour the passion fruit purée into a flute. Top with the Prosecco, give it a little stir, and serve.

DRINK
ROSSINI

SPECIAL

PROSECCO

ROSSINI

(Makes 1)

While you can find strawberries in grocery stores all year
round, there's really nothing so wonderful as that aromatic
moment in early summer when tiny, fresh local strawberries
are at their fleeting, seasonal peak. Always rinse them before
setting to work removing the green tops and cutting them up
for puréeing. This drink was named for the Italian composer
Rossini, whether because of his penchant for fine food and
drink, or for the bubbly character of his music, who can say.

Ingredients
1 fluid ounce Strawberry Purée (page 18)
3 fluid ounces extra dry-style Prosecco

Instructions
Pour the Strawberry Purée into a flute. Top with the Prosecco,
give it a little stir, and serve.

AUTUMN BELLINI

(Makes 1)

There's always a ton of talk about what wine to serve
for the eat-until-you-pop Thanksgiving holiday. But I
like to make sure I start my family and friends off with
something festive when they walk in the door; something
that makes them smile, slow down, and get in the
holiday mood. This easy-peasy, spicy, sparkling cocktail
makes a great kick-off to any epic celebration.

Ingredients
1 fluid ounce Spiced Pear Purée (page 18)
3 fluid ounces extra dry-style Prosecco
1 slender slice of pear, for garnish

Instructions
Pour the Spiced Pear Purée into a flute. Top with the Prosecco.
Give it a little stir and garnish with the pear slice.

SOUTHERN LIFE

(Makes 1)

Sweet Marsala (and, well, the dry version, too), from the area surrounding the eponymous city in Sicily, got kind of a bad rep for a while. You know, it became the kind of thing grannies drank from tiny glasses when they were feeling a little special. Well, with age comes wisdom—Marsala is delicious—and a multitude of bartenders have discovered its layered, complex charms in cocktails the world over. This southern Italian specialty, with its aromas and flavors of walnuts and dried fruit, adds a sophisticated note to the basic ingredients of a Bellini—peach purée and Prosecco (see page 27).

Ingredients
1 fluid ounce White Peach Purée (page 18)
¾ fluid ounce sweet Marsala wine
3 fluid ounces extra brut-style Prosecco

Instructions
Pour the White Peach Purée into a tulip glass. Add the Marsala and top with the Prosecco. Give it a little stir to keep the purée from settling on the bottom of the glass and serve.

FRAGOLA FIZZ

(Makes 1)

The key to this drink is giving your strawberries a good mashing—because you'll be sipping it with a straw, you don't want any getting stuck on the way up, so make sure you get all those solid pieces beneath your muddler! The fruitiness natural to Prosecco takes all those delicious strawberry aromatics and flavors to another level.

Ingredients
4 medium (or 3 large) strawberries, quartered
½ fluid ounce Mint Simple Syrup (page 16)
½ fluid ounce freshly squeezed lemon juice
1 fluid ounce vodka
3–4 fluid ounces brut-style Prosecco

Instructions
Drop the strawberries into a collins glass, pour in the Mint Simple Syrup, and muddle until very pulpy. Add the lemon juice and vodka. Fill with ice, top with the Prosecco, and give it a little stir to evenly distribute the mashed-up berries. Finish with a straw.

CLIMB EVERY MOUNTAIN

(Makes 1)

Pisco is a South American brandy made in both Peru and Chile that's distilled from crushed, fermented grapes (up to eight kinds in the mix!). Its calling card is the delightful Pisco Sour—a frothy frolic of a cocktail composed of Pisco, lime juice, simple syrup, egg white, and a swirl of Angostura bitters. But brandy and Prosecco? Oh, they like each other a lot, perhaps because they both have grapes at their core. Mix with a little orange-y, bittersweet Amaro Montenegro liqueur, and it makes for a fine low-alcohol, sophisticated sipper.

Ingredients
1 fluid ounce Pisco
¾ fluid ounce Amaro Montenegro liqueur
2 fluid ounces brut-style Prosecco
1 wide piece of orange peel, for garnish

Instructions
Pour the Pisco and Amaro Montenegro into an ice-filled double rocks glass. Stir well. Top with the Prosecco and garnish with the orange peel.

SBAGLIATO

(Makes 1)

Mistakes have a bad rep as being the result of a good thing gone wrong. But in the case of the *Sbagliato* (or "mistaken" in Italian), a wrong bottle made for a right cocktail. So the story goes: a bartender attempting to produce a hasty Negroni picked up a bottle of Prosecco instead of gin. And so, a lovely, lip-smacking aperitif was born. Although a Negroni calls for equal parts of its ingredients, I like to add a little more Prosecco to mine.

Ingredients
1 fluid ounce Campari
1 fluid ounce sweet vermouth
2 fluid ounces brut-style Prosecco
1 wide piece of orange peel, for garnish

Instructions
Pour the Campari, sweet vermouth, and Prosecco into an ice-filled double rocks glass. Give it a little stir and garnish with the orange peel.

SBAGLIATO 2

(Makes 1)

When the snow melts and the weather starts to turn a little nice, my husband often makes requests for cocktails that have a little fizz to them. He's a Negroni devotee, and one night when I was mixing one for myself, I offered him the same. "It sounds nice," he said, "but… I kinda want something with a little effervescence to it; a little pop." If a Sbagliato was indeed the result of a Negroni gone awry, why not put it back on the proper path and just add a little sparkle? It's become a hit around our house when a stirred drink needs just a little oomph on a Friday night.

Ingredients

¾ fluid ounce Campari
¾ fluid ounce sweet vermouth
¾ fluid ounce gin
1 fluid ounce brut-style Prosecco
1 wide piece of orange peel, for garnish

Instructions

Pour the Campari, sweet vermouth, gin, and Prosecco into an ice-filled double rocks glass. Give it a little stir and garnish with the orange peel.

SPARKLING CRUSTA

(Makes 1)

New Orleans, Louisiana is the birthplace of some of the world's best cocktails—the Sazerac, the Vieux Carre, the Ramos Gin Fizz, the Brandy Crusta. The latter offers up a whole lot of flavor and the sweet treat of a sugared rim, making it a great brunch, party, or post-dinner sipper. I like to play up the fruitiness of the Cognac with fig bitters instead of Angostura, as is traditional. Also, because there's a lot of liqueur components to this drink, I opt for a drier brut-style Prosecco to balance out the elements.

Ingredients

1½ fluid ounces Cognac VS
¼ fluid ounce Luxardo Maraschino liqueur
¼ fluid ounce triple sec
½ fluid ounce freshly squeezed lemon juice
   (reserving the squeezed out lemon)
¼ fluid ounce Simple Syrup (page 16)
2–3 dashes of fig bitters
1–2 fluid ounces brut-style Prosecco
Granulated sugar, to rim the glass
1 lemon twist, for garnish

Instructions

Combine the Cognac, Luxardo Maraschino liqueur, triple sec, lemon juice, Simple Syrup, and fig bitters in a shaker filled with ice and shake well. Rub the inside of the squeezed-out lemon around the rim of a coupe or cocktail glass. Sprinkle the sugar onto a flat plate and dip in the edges of the glass to coat the rim. Strain the contents of the shaker into the glass, top with Prosecco, and garnish with the lemon twist.

ITALIAN 75

(Makes 1)

Why should Champagne have all the fun? An elegant staple of the Sunday morning set, the French 75's origins are a bit murky (as many cocktail births are), but it seems to have had its pop-the-cork creation sometime during World War I. Another fogged-up lens into the past obscures whether the drink should be made with gin or Cognac, a debate that continues to rage. What is clear is that the 75 is unequivocal proof that the notion of adding sparkling (like in our souped-up Negroni on page 43) to a standard isn't a new idea, but a good one that's been in use for quite some time. For all intents and purposes, this drink begins as a sour, just one that gets a little extra zip via, in this case, Prosecco.

Ingredients

1½ fluid ounces Cognac
½ fluid ounce freshly squeezed lemon juice
½ fluid ounce Simple Syrup (page 16)
2 fluid ounces brut-style Prosecco
1 lemon twist, for garnish

Instructions

Pour the Cognac, lemon juice, and Simple Syrup into an ice-filled cocktail shaker. Shake well and strain into a coupe or cocktail glass. Top with the Prosecco and garnish with the lemon twist.

CHEERS TO SAL

(Makes 1)

New York City is full of southern Italian immigrants and their descendants who came by the millions between the 19th and 20th centuries (my own grandfather, grandmother, and aunts arrived in the 1920s, citizens already as my grandfather fought on the side of the Americans in World War I). My friend Tina's dad arrived toward the end of the great move of southern Italians and Sicilians to New York. One of his favorite things to sip on before dinner was a little Amaro Averna and Prosecco: a lovely bitter-fruity combo if there ever was one. The story goes that credit for the creation of Averna's liqueur is owed to Salvatore Averna, who was given the recipe by the monks of his local abbey in Caltanissetta, Sicily.

Ingredients
1½ fluid ounces Amaro Averna liqueur
3 fluid ounces extra dry-style Prosecco

Instructions
Pour the Averna into a flute and top with the Prosecco. Alternatively, you can also serve this over ice in a rocks glass.

SAL

NEW YORK

SICILIAN SPRITZ

(Makes 1)

I took the previous drink and tweaked it a little, using the concept of the spritz and Champagne cocktail to come up with something that I love to offer friends and guests to whet their appetites before dinner. I like using a brut-style Prosecco here, but if you prefer to tip this drink more toward the sweeter side, go for a dry style.

Ingredients
1 sugar cube
4–5 dashes of orange bitters
¾ fluid ounce Amaro Averna liqueur
2–3 fluid ounces brut-style Prosecco
Splash of club soda
1 wide piece of orange peel, for garnish

Instructions
Drop a sugar cube into a double rocks glass and splash it with the orange bitters. Crush with a muddler or a wooden spoon. Add the Amaro Averna, fill with ice, and pour in the Prosecco. Give it a little stir, top with a splash of club soda, and garnish with the orange peel.

CHERRY-OH

(Makes 1)

The inspiration for this drink came from the combo of kirsch (a brandy distilled from the fermented juice of morello cherries) and unsweetened black cherry juice—and how those two things seem to really sing when combined with a fruity Prosecco.

Ingredients
2 fluid ounces gin
2 fluid ounces unsweetened black cherry juice
½ fluid ounce kirsch
½ fluid ounce Simple Syrup (page 16)
1 drop of Peychaud's Bitters
1 fluid ounce extra dry-style Prosecco
1 morello cherry, for garnish

Instructions
Fill a cocktail shaker with ice. Pour in the gin, cherry juice, kirsch, Simple Syrup, and bitters. Shake well and strain into a coupe glass. Top with the Prosecco and garnish with a morello cherry.

GREEN EYES

(Makes 1)

The tart combination of citrusy-style gin, herbaceous Green Chartreuse and sprightly lemon juice gets a really fun bit of sparkle and sweetness from a fruity, dry-style Prosecco here and is a great way to usher in spring (or, perhaps, try to hurry it along!).

Ingredients

1 ½ fluid ounces gin
½ fluid ounce Green Chartreuse
¼ fluid ounce freshly squeezed lemon juice
2 fluid ounces dry-style Prosecco
1 thin slice of Granny Smith apple, for garnish

Instructions

Fill a cocktail shaker with ice. Pour in the gin, Chartreuse, and lemon juice. Shake well and strain into an ice-filled double rocks glass. Top with the Prosecco and garnish with the apple slice.

SHIP TO SHORE

(Makes 1)

My friend Kevin Rice is an architect. He and his awesome architect wife, Tina Vultaggio, live about three doors down from me and are, quite often, the guinea pigs for liquidy libations I'm attempting to concoct. Kevin also happens to be a pretty good co-creator of cocktails. Sometimes, if I'm just missing something, he can come up with an element that brings the whole thing together. This is one of those cocktails. It sounds like a crazy combo of items, but beneath it all there's this hum of rich ripe and dried fruits that get a boost from both the spicy habanero bitters and extra-dry Prosecco. The name? Rum, Cognac, and port historically spent a whole lot of time on boats.

Ingredients

½ fluid ounce Jamaican rum
½ fluid ounce Cognac
½ fluid ounce tawny port
¾ fluid ounce freshly squeezed lemon juice
1 teaspoon orange curaçao
¼ fluid ounce Simple Syrup (page 16)
1 dash of habanero bitters
1 fluid ounce extra dry-style Prosecco

Instructions

Fill a cocktail shaker with ice. Pour in the rum, Cognac, port, lemon juice, curaçao, Simple Syrup, and habanero bitters. Shake well and strain into a coupe or cocktail glass. Top with the Prosecco.

SHINY NAIL

(Makes 1)

My Dad, Michael Zavatto, introduced me to the charms
of this not very charmingly named cocktail (well, you
know, unless you have a thing for rusty nails). But its name
isn't because it's a tetanus-dispensing drink; it's for the
color that Drambuie (a honey-and-Scotch liqueur) draws
out in it, adding a pretty touch of browny-red to its hue.
With this drink, I think it's worth going for a DOCG-status
Prosecco from the Valdobbiadene area, where the rocky,
marine-deposit soils add a minerally, briny character
that fits the drink nicely. I like using a blended Scotch
that has a hint of salt and smoke with a fruity base, like
Cutty Sark, Famous Grouse, or Johnny Walker Red.

Ingredients
2½ fluid ounces Scotch
¼ fluid ounce Drambuie
2 fluid ounces extra dry-style Prosecco
1 wide piece of lemon peel, for garnish

Instructions
Fill a double rocks glass with ice. Pour in the
Scotch and Drambuie. Give it a little stir, top with
Prosecco, and garnish with the lemon peel.

FELICE'S FERRAGOSTO

(Makes 1)

A few years back, my husband and I went for a visit to my father-in-law's region of Sicily, Agrigento, during the summer celebration there known as Ferragosto (the Roman Catholic celebration that basically kicks off the summer holidays in Italy). After a long day on the beach, the towns come alive at night with music, street fairs, and throngs of vacationers strolling around, eating gelato, and enjoying the time off from work and school. One of our favorite things to do was grab a seat at an outdoor café within earshot of some live music, spooning out a chilly, espresso-topped affogato, or simply sipping on a little amaretto over ice. This drink brings me right back there.

Ingredients
1 fluid ounce amaretto liqueur
1 fluid ounce freshly squeezed orange juice
2 dashes of orange bitters
3 fluid ounces extra dry-style Prosecco
1 wide piece of orange peel, for garnish

Instructions
Pour the amaretto, orange juice, and bitters into an ice-filled double rocks glass and top with the Prosecco. Give it a little stir and garnish with the orange peel.

COME ON IN

(Makes 1)

I love the combination of fresh basil and pineapple.
A gently fruit-forward, extra dry- or dry-style Prosecco
boosts all that great sweet herby and tropical flavor even
more. Mionetto makes a non-vintage DOCG version
from Valdobbiadene from the town of Cartizze that has
the perfect combo of notes (floral, herby, and a touch
of kiwi-tropical fruit) that goes so nicely with this drink.
(The name? Pineapples are the symbol of welcome!)

Ingredients
1 ½ fluid ounces London dry gin
¼ fluid ounce Basil Syrup (page 16)
2 fluid ounces unsweetened pineapple juice
2 dashes of lemon bitters
3 fluid ounces extra dry- or dry-style Prosecco
1 sprig of basil, for garnish
1 pineapple wedge, for garnish

Instructions
Pour the gin, Basil Syrup, pineapple juice, and lemon bitters
into a cocktail shaker filled with ice. Shake well and strain
into a collins glass. Top with the Prosecco, garnish with a
sprig of basil and a pineapple wedge, and pop in a straw.

POSITANO POP

(Makes 1)

Italy's picturesque Amalfi Coast has earned its reputation as a vacation dream spot, with its dramatic cliffs jutting from the Sorrentine Peninsula and pretty little beaches—and, of course, ever-flowing bottles of potent, sweet-tart limoncello. This twist on a Champagne cocktail swaps out the Cognac with Positano's popular digestif.

Ingredients
1 sugar cube
4–5 drops of lemon bitters
¾ fluid ounce limoncello
3 fluid ounces brut-style Prosecco
1 lemon twist, for garnish

Instructions
Drop the sugar cube into a Champagne flute. Saturate with the lemon bitters and then break it up using a muddler or the end of a wooden spoon. Pour in the limoncello and top with the Prosecco. Garnish with the lemon twist.

BUBBLY JACK ROSE

(Makes 1)

Brandy and Prosecco are easy friends. You can riff on the two ingredients adding in other layers of flavor with little fear of failure. The Jack Rose is a great American cocktail that makes good use of something called Applejack—American apple brandy made popular during the colonial era. The gentle presence of residual sugar in an extra dry-level Prosecco works well here to put a bit of fruity sparkle on top of this classic cocktail— and if you really want to fine-tune the flavors, I'm a fan of working with an extra dry-style DOCG version from the Rive di Manzana in Conegliano (Frasinelli's works great), with its rich mouthfeel and orchard-fruit notes.

Ingredients

1½ fluid ounces Applejack
¼ fluid ounce Grenadine (page 17)
½ fluid ounce freshly squeezed lemon juice
2 fluid ounces extra dry-style Prosecco
1 lemon twist, for garnish

Instructions

Pour the Applejack, Grenadine, and lemon juice into a cocktail shaker filled with ice. Shake well and strain into a coupe or cocktail glass. Top with the Prosecco and garnish with the lemon twist.

GARDEN WALK

(Makes 1)

Lemon verbena is one of my favorite potted herbs to grow because its aroma is absolutely irresistible and its fast, prolific growth is totally just-add-water rewarding. Its lemony-sweet smell kind of reminds me of Juicy Fruit chewing gum, and it makes the most delicious simple syrup in the world (see page 16 for instructions on how to make simple syrups). Combine it with some gin, a brut-style Prosecco, and some celery bitters and you won't know what's more pleasurable—sniffing its pretty aromatics or sipping this lovely refreshing combo. Okay, sipping.

Ingredients

1¾ fluid ounces gin
½ fluid ounce lemon verbena syrup
½ fluid ounce freshly squeezed lemon juice
2 dashes of celery bitters
3 fluid ounces brut-style Prosecco
1 lemon slice or lemon verbena sprig, for garnish

Instructions

Pour the gin, lemon verbena syrup, lemon juice, and celery bitters into a cocktail shaker filled with ice. Shake well and strain into an ice-filled collins glass. Top with the Prosecco. Garnish with a lemon slice or sprig of lemon verbena (or, heck, both!) and pop in a straw.

SEEDS OF CHANGE

(Makes 1)

The sweet-tart taste of pomegranate goes gorgeously with a dry, brut-style Prosecco (it's also a great start to a sparkling punch if you need to throw one together in a jiffy!). Think of this as a revved-up Mimosa.

Ingredients
A few pomegranate seeds
1 fluid ounce vodka
¾ fluid ounce pomegranate liqueur (I use PAMA)
¾ fluid ounce freshly squeezed orange juice
3 fluid ounces brut-style Prosecco

Instructions
Drop a few pomegranate seeds into a flute.
Pour in the vodka, pomegranate liqueur, and orange juice and top with the Prosecco.

DANCE PARTY

(Makes 1)

There are drinks that just go down so easy, they seem to have powers beyond simply tasting delicious. Like, say, one minute you're sipping on this little rum-based Prosecco charmer and the next thing you know you and all your buds are dancing round your living room. This floral, fun, citrusy sparkler promises to do just that.

Ingredients

1 ½ fluid ounces white rum
¾ fluid ounce elderflower liqueur
½ fluid ounce freshly squeezed lime juice
2 fluid ounces brut-style Prosecco
1 wide piece of lime peel, for garnish

Instructions

Fill a cocktail shaker with ice. Pour in the rum, elderflower liqueur, and lime juice. Shake well and strain into an ice-filled double rocks glass. Top with the Prosecco and garnish with the lime peel.

TIZIANO

(Makes 1)

Invented in Venice, this sparkling cocktail uses muddled black grapes to create its color (the inspiration for its name, the 16th-century painter Tiziano Vecellio, was fond of the purplish-red hue that the cocktail's main ingredient adds). Where I live, Concord grapes are prolific and easy to find in the late summer and early autumn, so I use them to make a syrup that adds a fun local twist to this Italian tipple (although any red or black grapes will do).

Ingredients
1 fluid ounce Concord Grape Syrup (page 17)
3–4 fluid ounces brut-style Prosecco

Instructions
Pour the grape syrup into a flute. Top with the Prosecco.

GRAND AVENUE FROLIC

(Makes 1)

In the town I grew up in, there is an old hotel called the Chequit that used to be the site of a great bar where lots and lots of merrymaking occurred on a nightly basis all summer long. It was the 80s. There was lots of neon, asymmetrical hair, Depeche Mode, dancing, and drinking of bright, tropical, summery things, like the Madras—a particularly popular tipple among my friends and me. I abandoned it as years went on for less fruity, more "serious" cocktails. But the thing is, who wants to be so serious when sipping cocktails? Especially bubbly ones. This souped-up Madras is even more delicious with a splash of extra-dry Prosecco. Viva la 80s.

Ingredients
1 ½ fluid ounces vodka
¾ fluid ounce cranberry juice
¾ fluid ounce freshly squeezed orange juice
1 fluid ounce freshly squeezed lime juice
½ fluid ounce Cointreau
3 fluid ounces extra dry-style Prosecco
1 wide piece of lime peel, for garnish

Instructions
Fill a cocktail shaker with ice. Pour in the vodka, cranberry juice, orange and lime juices, and Cointreau. Shake well and strain into an ice-filled collins glass. Top with the Prosecco, garnish with the lime peel, and pop in a straw.

MIMOSA SUD

(Makes 1)

Perhaps one of the easiest cocktails to throw together is that classic brunch staple, the Mimosa. Orange juice, sparkling, boom! You're done. But not only that, you've got something refreshing and festive that never fails to put a smile on everyone's face. Taking a little extra effort though, in the form of squeezing some fresh juice, makes a world of difference. Here, I like to add a little Italian twist with fresh blood orange juice, for both its flavor and gorgeous color, along with an extra dry-style Prosecco to add a nice, round fruitiness to the sparkle and pop.

Ingredients
2 fluid ounces freshly squeezed blood orange juice
3–4 fluid ounces brut-style Prosecco

Instructions
Pour the blood orange juice into a flute. Top with the Prosecco.

RISE OF THE MOJITO

(Makes 1)

Adding a little Prosecco in place of the usual club soda in a Mojito makes this perennial fun favorite even more refreshing (and aromatic!). Definitely veer toward a drier-style Prosecco with a little more minerality (think DOCG Valdobbiadene), as it livens up and plays well with all that fresh, fragrant mint.

Ingredients

7–8 fresh mint leaves, plus an extra sprig for garnish

¾ fluid ounce Simple Syrup (page 16)

¾ fluid ounce freshly squeezed lime juice

2 fluid ounces white rum

3 fluid ounces extra dry-style Prosecco

Instructions

Drop the mint leaves into a cocktail shaker and top with the Simple Syrup. Muddle until the leaves release their natural oils and you start to smell all that nice minty freshness. Add in some ice. Pour in the lime juice and rum and shake well. Strain into an ice-filled collins glass. Top with the Prosecco, garnish with the mint sprig, and pop in a straw.

PUCCINI

(Makes 1)

You know it's the festive season when bags and small wooden crates of clementines begin to appear at your local grocery stores. They are a smaller, sweeter, seedless offshoot of a mandarin orange, which is the source of citrus for this Northern Italian-created sipper. The inventor of this drink was, apparently, one Renato Haussmann, a barman who crafted a new version of the Mimosa during the winter of 1948 in the alpine city of Cortina d'Ampezzo at the Posta Hotel. The name is for Giacomo Puccini; the citrus for the eponymous mandarin heroine of his opera, *Turandot*. I prefer to switch out the traditional flute for a tulip glass in order to really get a whiff of those lovely clementine aromatics, and use a brut-style Prosecco as clementines are naturally super sweet.

Ingredients
2 fluid ounces freshly squeezed clementine juice
3-4 fluid ounces brut-style Prosecco

Instructions
Pour the fresh clementine juice into a tulip glass. Top with the Prosecco.

OF COURSE

(Makes 1)

Marinating melon in sweet Marsala wine adds a sweet-savory kick to the fruit. I like to use honeydew for this recipe, but feel free to use your favorite melon (or whatever kind you happen to have in your house at the time).

Ingredients
1 cup honeydew melon, cut up into cubes
4 fluid ounces sweet Marsala wine
3 fluid ounces extra dry-style Prosecco

Instructions
Place the melon pieces in a bowl and pour the Marsala wine over them. Cover and refrigerate for 2–4 hours. Purée the mixture in a blender or food processor (you will have more than enough for several drinks; store any extra in a glass, airtight container for a day or two). Pour 2 fluid ounces of the mixture into a tulip glass and top with the Prosecco.

THE SEELBACH

(Makes 1)

Who says whiskey and bubbles can't be friends? This lovely whiskey-centric drink was created by barman Adam Seger in 1995 to provide its namesake hotel (given a spot of fame for its mention by F. Scott Fitzgerald in *The Great Gatsby*) in Louisville, Kentucky, with a much-needed signature cocktail. The result made this drink a classic far and beyond its late-20th-century birth.

Ingredients

1 fluid ounce Old Forester bourbon (or your favorite brand)
½ fluid ounce triple sec
7 dashes of Angostura bitters
7 dashes of Peychaud's Bitters
3–4 fluid ounces brut-style Prosecco
1 orange twist, for garnish

Instructions

Fill a cocktail shaker with ice. Pour in the bourbon, triple sec, and bitters. Stir well and strain into a flute. Top with the Prosecco and garnish with the orange twist.

ROSABEL

(Makes 1)

Taking a cue from the Kir Royale, a Rosabel uses Prosecco more as a way of unifying the crème de cassis and sweet vermouth rather than highlighting the sparkling, but this pretty red-hued, low-alcohol drink is a great way to kick off, or even end, an evening. Although the traditional way of serving it is in a flute, I prefer this drink over ice with a nice, wide swath of orange peel.

Ingredients

1 fluid ounce crème de cassis
1 fluid ounce Cocchi Vermouth di Torino
¾ fluid ounce brut-style Prosecco
1 wide piece of orange peel, for garnish

Instructions

Combine the crème de cassis and vermouth in an ice-filled double rocks glass. Give it a little stir and top with the Prosecco. Garnish with the orange peel.

PINK SGROPPINO

(Makes 1)

It's summer. It's hot. It's sticky! What you need is internal air-conditioning. You can play around with the sweetness level on this chilly, fruity, kicked-up adult treat depending on where and when you want to have it (before dinner as a palate cleanser, or after as dessert) and change the sorbet flavor for your favorite kind. I like the fun, fruity kick of raspberries here combined with a sweeter-style (aka, dry) Prosecco for an afternoon treat or post-barbecue cap-off.

Ingredients
½ cup raspberry sorbet
¾ fluid ounce Gewürztraminer grappa
3 fluid ounces dry-style Prosecco
3–4 fresh raspberries, for garnish

Instructions
Place the sorbet, Prosecco, and grappa in a cocktail shaker and shake until combined and smooth. Pour into a tulip glass and garnish with the fresh raspberries.

SPARKLING BONAPARTE

(Makes 1)

Prosecco and Cognac really, really like each other. Maybe it's because they are cousins in grape-based beginnings; maybe it's just that sparkling wine highlights the fruit-centric notes in great brandy. I like the combo here of Cognac and Prosecco with pink grapefruit juice and the underlying orange-y hum of Cointreau.

Ingredients
¾ fluid ounce Cognac VS
½ fluid ounce Cointreau
1 fluid ounce freshly squeezed pink grapefruit juice
1–2 fluid ounces extra dry-style Prosecco

Instructions
Fill a cocktail shaker with ice. Pour in the Cognac, Cointreau, and pink grapefruit juice. Shake well and strain into a coupe glass. Top with the Prosecco.

BREAK THE SILENCE

(Makes 1)

One of the most pivotal screen stars of the 20th century, Charlie Chaplin, somehow managed to make a big impression without uttering a sound. This riff on his namesake cocktail breaks the silence with the festive pop of a Prosecco cork (and, perhaps, the slurp of a straw at the bottom of a glass—it's just that delicious!).

Ingredients

1½ fluid ounces sloe gin
½ fluid ounce apricot brandy
1 fluid ounce freshly squeezed lime juice
½ fluid ounce Simple Syrup (page 16)
1–2 fluid ounces brut-style Prosecco

Instructions

Fill a cocktail shaker with ice. Pour in the sloe gin, apricot brandy, lime juice, and Simple Syrup. Shake well and strain into a coupe or cocktail glass. Top with the Prosecco.

GROWN-UP LEMONADE

(Makes 1)

This drink is a tiny bit dangerous—it's so refreshing and easy to drink, you'll find it disappears fast. Use a good-quality limoncello (Caravella makes a nice version), or plan ahead (a week to 10 days for maceration) and make your own!

Ingredients

1¼ fluid ounces vodka

¾ fluid ounce limoncello

3 dashes of lemon bitters

2–3 fluid ounces brut-style Prosecco

1 wide piece of lemon peel, for garnish

Instructions

Fill a double rocks glass with ice. Pour in the vodka, limoncello, and bitters. Give it a good stir. Top with the Prosecco and garnish with the lemon peel.

NATURE, NURTURE
(Makes 1)

Your in-laws are coming over for lunch. You want to
show them you're sophisticated, but also interesting.
And fun. In other words, you want to give them a glimpse
of why their precious offspring has fallen for you. Avoid
discussing politics and have one of these at the ready
when they walk in the door. It's delicious and refreshing,
but the cucumber-tinged Hendrick's, bright addition of
lime bitters, and pretty sparkle from a brut-style Prosecco
make it more interesting than simply gin and juice.

Ingredients
1½ fluid ounces Hendrick's gin
¾ fluid ounce elderflower liqueur
2 fluid ounces unsweetened pineapple juice
2 dashes of lime bitters
2–3 fluid ounces brut-style Prosecco
1 wide piece of lime peel, for garnish

Instructions
Fill a shaker with ice. Pour in the gin, elderflower liqueur,
pineapple juice, and lime bitters. Give it a good shake
and strain into an ice-filled double rocks glass. Top
with the Prosecco and garnish with the lime peel.

FIZZY WATERMELON MARGARITA

(Makes 1)

Watermelon has got to be one of the most thirst-quenching fruits in the entire world. And actually, its name is no accident: the brightly-hued fruit is 92% water. But I don't have to tell you that despite the water, it's not without flavor—and, in this case, flavor that gets wonderfully kicked up with a little extra dry-style Prosecco.

Ingredients

3 fluid ounces Watermelon Purée (page 18)
1 fluid ounce silver tequila
½ fluid ounce triple sec
¾ fluid ounce freshly squeezed lime juice
½ fluid ounce Simple Syrup (page 16)
2 fluid ounces extra dry-style Prosecco
3 frozen watermelon cubes, for garnish
1 fresh mint sprig, for garnish

Instructions

Combine the Watermelon Purée, tequila, triple sec, lime juice, and Simple Syrup in a shaker filled with ice. Shake well and strain into an ice-filled double rocks glass. Top with the Prosecco. Skewer the frozen watermelon cubes onto a single toothpick and garnish with this and the mint sprig.

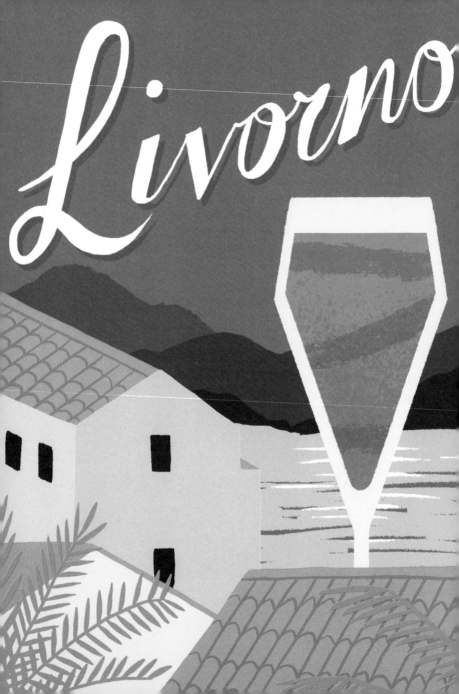

LEGHORN SPRITZ

(Makes 1)

Sunny yellow and presented in a gorgeous, tall, slim glass bottle, Galliano got quite a bit of mid-20th-century fame for the once-popular Harvey Wallbanger cocktail. But this exotic, sweet, herbaceous liqueur's history goes all the way back to 1896, when it was invented by the brandy producer Arturo Vaccari in the Tuscan city of Livorno, who named it for Giuseppe Galliano, a hero of the Italo-Ethiopian War. For reasons I have yet to uncover, Brits like to refer to this city on the Ligurian Sea as Leghorn. But while that might be a mystery, the delicious combo of the lo-fi ingredients below is not.

Ingredients

¾ fluid ounce Galliano liqueur

¾ fluid ounce Aperol

3 fluid ounces brut-style Prosecco

1 wide piece of lemon peel, for garnish

Instructions

Pour the Galliano and Aperol into an ice-filled double rocks glass. Give it a little stir and top with the Prosecco. Garnish with the lemon peel.

SUNSHINE SUPERMAN

(Makes 1)

One evening, my husband Dan came home after a particularly stressful, horrible work day and the look on his face said to me, oh dear, that man needs something to put a smile on his face. And rum? Well, if rum can't put you in a better mood, I don't know what can. I had a little leftover ice wine from a dinner party, and was struck by inspiration: the caramelized, vanilla, dried fruit flavors in the rum combined with the apricot notes of the ice wine and the bright, buoyant fruit in a dry-style Prosecco sounded like just the trick. It was! Spouse happy, new favorite cocktail created. Win-win.

Ingredients
1½ fluid ounces Jamaican rum
½ fluid ounce ice wine (see below)
1 fluid ounce brut-style Prosecco
1 wide piece of orange peel, for garnish

Instructions
Pour the rum and ice wine into an ice-filled double rocks glass. Give it a little stir and top with the Prosecco. Garnish with the orange peel.

Ice wine is exactly what it sounds like—it's made from grapes left on their vines long after the normal harvest time so that they literally freeze. When this happens, the sugars inside them become more concentrated and almost honey-like, so when they are quickly crushed after picking, the result is a near-syrupy, decadent dessert wine that will make you swoon.

BORDER PASS

(Makes 1)

I like a Paloma as much, or possibly even more, than a Margarita. It's so simple and makes ample use of grapefruit juice (a plus in my book!). This souped-up version adds a little lime and simple syrup, along with a bubbly burst of dry-style Prosecco.

Ingredients

1 fluid ounce freshly squeezed grapefruit juice
¼ fluid ounce freshly squeezed lime juice
1½ fluid ounces reposado tequila
½ fluid ounce Simple Syrup (page 16)
3 fluid ounces dry-style Prosecco

Instructions

Fill a shaker with ice. Pour in the grapefruit juice, lime juice, tequila, and Simple Syrup. Shake well and strain into an ice-filled collins glass. Top with the Prosecco and add a straw.

ISLAY SOUR

(Makes 1)

One recent spring evening on an unseasonably hot day where I live in New York, I had some pink grapefruit sitting around in the refrigerator. I was trying to figure out what to make to go with some fish I had for dinner and considered putting the grapefruit on the grill—it caramelizes the sugars and makes a nice smoky-sweet accent. But then I got to thinking: wouldn't it be cool to make a refreshing drink that emulated that smoky grapefruit flavor using mezcal or Islay Scotch? The answer was yes, yes it was! The drink on its own is lovely, but add a splash of brut-style Prosecco, and the flavors are really lifted up. I prefer the single malt Uigeadail from the wonderful Ardbeg distillery in Islay, because its strong smoke component is beautifully balanced by a rich, fruity characteristic in the malt.

Ingredients
1 fluid ounce Ardbeg "Uigeadail" single malt Scotch
1 fluid ounce pink grapefruit juice
¼ fluid ounce Simple Syrup (page 16)
1–2 fluid ounces brut-style Prosecco
1 wide piece of pink grapefruit peel, for garnish

Instructions
Fill a cocktail shaker with ice cubes. Pour in the Scotch, grapefruit juice, and Simple Syrup. Shake for 20 seconds. Strain slowly into an ice-filled double rocks glass. Top with the Prosecco and garnish with the grapefruit peel.

SUNDAY IN THE PARK

(Makes 1)

The delicate, soft floral notes of chamomile combined
with a brut-style Prosecco make such a lovely combo,
all they really need are some subtle accents via a little
Cointreau and a touch of ginger. Combine the first three
ingredients in a chilled thermos, grab a bottle of Prosecco,
and bring this concoction to your next picnic in the park.

Ingredients
3 fluid ounces unsweetened chamomile tea
½ fluid ounce Cointreau
¼ fluid ounce Ginger Simple Syrup (page 17)
3 fluid ounces extra dry-style Prosecco
1 slice of fresh peach or orange, for garnish

Instructions
Fill a collins glass with ice. Pour in the tea, Cointreau,
and Ginger Simple Syrup. Stir for a few seconds and
top with the Prosecco. Pop in a straw and garnish
with a thin slice of fresh peach or orange.

TODAY'S WINNER

(Makes 1)

This twist on a classic Brandy Crusta gets its little tropical update from some unsweetened pineapple juice and tiki bitters, which, depending on the producer, tend to have an exotic edge to them, with spices and notes of cinnamon, allspice, ginger, and citrus. Combined with an extra dry-style Prosecco, this winner of a sipper will take your taste buds swiftly over the finish line.

Ingredients
1½ fluid ounces Cognac
¼ fluid ounce Luxardo Maraschino liqueur
¼ fluid ounce triple sec
¼ fluid ounce freshly squeezed lemon juice
½ fluid ounce unsweetened pineapple juice
3 dashes of tiki bitters
2 fluid ounces extra dry-style Prosecco
1 strawberry, for garnish

Instructions
Combine the Cognac, Maraschino liqueur, triple sec, lemon juice, pineapple juice, and tiki bitters in an ice-filled shaker. Shake well and strain into a tulip glass. Top with the Prosecco and garnish with a strawberry.

LUXE LIFE

(Makes 1)

If your only familiarity with the word "maraschino" is of the unnaturally red, super-sweet cherries that top a sundae, you're in for a big treat. Maraschino liqueur is distilled from marasca cherries, stones and all. The final result is a beautiful, brandy-like beauty that smells like pretty flowers and nuts—and is Prosecco's absolute best buddy in the glass. No lie. Maybe even more than Cognac. So much so, you really don't need anything else with it, the two together are such a great combo. Pop in another one of Italy's famed cherries as a garnish, and you've got an easy, impressive cocktail to quickly serve a crowd. With a two-ingredient cocktail such as this one, it may be worth your while to upgrade to a DOCG Prosecco. Seek out one from the eastern part of the DOCG, where the soils encourage more of a stone fruit and mineral profile in the wine.

Ingredients
1 Amarena cherry
1 fluid ounce Luxardo Maraschino liqueur
3–4 fluid ounces extra dry-style Prosecco

Instructions
Drop the cherry into a flute. Pour in the Luxardo Maraschino liqueur and top with the Prosecco.

AIR MAIL

(Makes 1)

If you've never had the pleasure of flipping through
Esquire's *Handbook for Hosts* (first published in 1949;
revisited in 1977), you're in for a time-warp treat.
Not only is it chock-full of hostess-with-the-mostest
recipes, advice on equipment, and a funny picture of
a naked lady, it also offers up coin tricks to entertain
your guests and drink recipes like this little gem.

Ingredients
2 fluid ounces golden rum
¾ fluid ounce freshly squeezed lime juice
½ fluid ounce Honey Syrup (page 17)
3–4 fluid ounces brut-style Prosecco
1 lime twist, for garnish

Instructions
Combine the rum, lime juice, and Honey Syrup in an ice-
filled shaker. Shake well and strain into an ice-filled collins
glass. Top with the Prosecco and garnish with a lime twist.

COUNTESS CRAWLEY

(Makes 1)

Oh, Countess Crawley. You of the high-stacked hair and demure Victorian dresses. But while the Countess is ever the straight-backed, pursed-lipped arbiter of manners and good taste, beneath that buttoned-up, feather-accented, begloved exterior is the woman who had an affair with a Russian prince. That Countess? She'd like a genteel little cocktail with her name on it. A little dose of lavender-hued crème de violette, fresh lemon, and sprightly Prosecco seems just the trick.

Ingredients

¾ fluid ounce crème de violette

¾ fluid ounce freshly squeezed lemon juice

1 fluid ounce gin (for this recipe, I prefer something floral, such as NY Distilling's Dorothy Parker American Gin)

2 fluid ounces extra dry-style Prosecco

1 blackberry, for garnish

Instructions

Combine the crème de violette, lemon juice, and gin in an ice-filled shaker. Shake well and strain into a tulip glass. Top with the Prosecco and garnish with a blackberry.

HOW BLUE AM I

(Makes 1)

I wrote my book, *Forager's Cocktails*, because I suspected
that there were a lot of people like me out there: that is, folks
who are brave enough to pick up stinging nettles to see what
they might inspire, but also those who really relish what to me
is the kernel of the whole idea—using fresh, in-season items,
be they from a woodland hike or a safari through your local
farmer's market. You can forage for wild blueberries not
too far from where I live, but you can also nab some pretty
nice ones at the grocery store. And picking off a handful of
fresh basil leaves? Ahhh—such a beautiful scent and totally
great combo with the fruit, lemon juice, and Prosecco!

Ingredients
¼ cup fresh blueberries, plus 3–4 for garnish, rinsed
½ fluid ounce Basil Simple Syrup (page 16)
1½ fluid ounces vodka
¾ fluid ounce freshly squeezed lemon juice
3 fluid ounces brut-style Prosecco

Instructions
Drop the blueberries into a shaker. Add the Simple Syrup
and muddle thoroughly. Fill with ice, add the vodka and
lemon juice, and shake well. Strain through a fine mesh
sieve into an ice-filled double rocks glass. Top with the
Prosecco and garnish with the remaining blueberries.

TEQUILA SUNRISE & SHINE

(Makes 1)

Like the Old Fashioned and other cocktails that were invented at the turn of, or early part of the 20th century, the Tequila Sunrise's original demure combo of tequila, crème de cassis, lime juice, and club soda got entirely lost in the shuffle of the sweet and lowdown 70s. Swap the club soda for a brut-style Prosecco and this classic cocktail sparkles even brighter from the first sip.

Ingredients

1 ½ fluid ounces silver tequila

¾ fluid ounce crème de cassis

½ fluid ounce freshly squeezed lime juice

2–3 fluid ounces brut-style Prosecco

1 lime twist, for garnish

Instructions

Combine the tequila, crème de cassis, and lime juice in an ice-filled shaker. Shake well and strain into an ice-filled double rocks glass. Top with the Prosecco and garnish with the lime twist.

70s TEQUILA SUNRISE

(Makes 1)

Now, before you go kicking the popularized sweet 'n sticky version of the Tequila Sunrise to the curb, consider instead just giving it a little fresh intervention. High-fructose corn syrup juices and mixers? Ick. Grab a couple of oranges, mix up some easy-peasy homemade grenadine, and take the shame out of that Sunrise. With a little brut-style Prosecco (going dry in sparkling style here adds some nice balance to the drink's inherent fruitiness), this updated 70s sipper becomes a whole new modern-day hit.

Ingredients
1½ fluid ounces reposado tequila
2 fluid ounces freshly squeezed orange juice
¼ fluid ounce Grenadine (page 17)
2–3 fluid ounces brut-style Prosecco
1 orange slice, for garnish

Instructions
Pour the tequila, orange juice, and Grenadine into an ice-filled highball glass. Give it a good stir and top with the Prosecco. Garnish with an orange slice and pop in a straw.

FELIX'S OTHER FIZZ

(Makes 1)

The classic Kir cocktail was invented by, and subsequently named after, the Canon Felix Kir, mayor of Burgundy and champion of all the delicious things that come from that lovely area of France, like crème de cassis and the traditional Kir (that uses a still white wine made from the grape Aligote). Swap out the latter for a little sparkly Cremant de Bourgogne, and you've got yourself a Kir Royale. And as long as we're riffing, Prosecco makes a pretty lovely substitute—just make sure you go with a brut style, as the cocktail is not meant to be sweet. And if you can find yourself a bottle of extra brut-style? Go for it! Your refreshed senses will thank you.

Ingredients
¼ fluid ounce crème de cassis
4 fluid ounces brut- or extra brut-style Prosecco
1 raspberry, for garnish

Instructions
Pour the crème de cassis into a flute. Top with the Prosecco and garnish with a raspberry.

KIWI COOLER

(Makes 1)

The soft, fleshy texture of kiwi fruit responds well to a little time in the freezer. Whiz it up with a gin like Hendrick's (with its pretty cucumber and floral notes) and a little mint simple syrup, top with a glug of extra dry-style Prosecco, and you have a super-chilly, sparkly cooler ripe for the quenching.

Ingredients

4 kiwi slices, just frozen (about 1 kiwi),
   plus 1 unfrozen slice for garnish
½ fluid ounce Mint Simple Syrup (page 16)
¼ fluid ounce freshly squeezed lime juice
1 fluid ounce Hendrick's gin
2–3 fluid ounces extra dry-style Prosecco
1 fresh mint sprig, for garnish

Instructions

Remove the kiwi slices from the freezer when they are just starting to harden. Drop in a blender or food processer with the Mint Syrup and lime juice, and blend until smooth. Strain through a fine-mesh sieve and pour into a tulip glass. Top with the Prosecco and garnish with a slice of kiwi and a mint sprig.

KEY PUNCH

(Serves 12 to 14)

Every winter, I head down to Key West, Florida, at the southernmost tip of the United States. When you fly in over the blue gulf, looking at the sailboats dotting the water and all the little islands (or keys) that lead up to Key West, any stress that you might have carried with you onto the plane drops right off once the wheels hit the ground among the swaying palms and hilarious famed crowing roosters. It's the kind of place, with its abundance of the petite Key Lime fruit, that makes you thoroughly understand why Ernest Hemingway found his way down there and lingered. The following is my riff on a large-format Hemingway Daiquiri—with bubbles, because Key West is nothing if not a super fun town.

Ingredients
1 ice ring (page 19)
1 cup white rum
½ cup triple sec
½ cup freshly squeezed lime juice
2 cups unsweetened pineapple juice
½ cup Simple Syrup (page 16)
1 (750 milliliter) bottle of extra dry-style Prosecco
1 lime, sliced into thin rings

Instructions
Place the ice ring into a punch bowl. Combine the first 5 ingredients. Give them a gentle stir. Pour in the Prosecco. Garnish with lime slices. Ladle into punch cups and serve.

CHRISTMAS BRUNCH PUNCH

(Serves 12 to 14)

Red, bubbly, and entirely festive, this spicy punch is the perfect crowd-pleaser, whether you're inviting family and friends into your own home (which, really, is the genius of punch—it keeps you from having to constantly worry about ingredients for a million different mixed drinks), or looking for something to take to a party you're attending to help your host enjoy the party, too!

Ingredients

1 ice ring (page 19)
½ cup pomegranate liqueur (I use PAMA)
2 cups pomegranate juice
½ cup pear juice
½ cup freshly squeezed lemon juice
¼ cup Cinnamon Simple Syrup (page 17)
1 (750 milliliter) bottle of brut-style Prosecco
Fresh pomegranate seeds, for garnish

Instructions

Place the ice ring into a punch bowl. Combine the first 5 ingredients. Give them a gentle stir. Pour in the Prosecco. Garnish with the pomegranate seeds. Ladle into punch cups and serve.

A great way to make this punch even more festive is to wet the rim of 12 to 14 rocks glasses with lemon juice (use the lemons you squeezed for the juice). Combine ½ cup sugar with 1 tablespoon ground cinnamon on a flat plate, and dip the rims of the glasses in the sugar mixture. Let dry and set out for your guests to fill with punch.

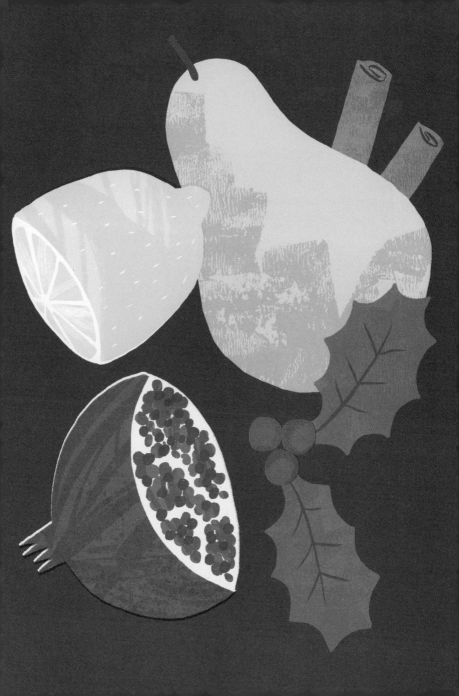

FIZZY LEMONADE PUNCH

(Serves 12 to 14)

Great for an afternoon party or Sunday brunch with friends. Whip up this easy, lemony punch to impress a crowd without having to put in very much effort!

Ingredients
1 ice ring (page 19)
2 cups gin
1 cup freshly squeezed lemon juice
¼ fluid ounce orange flower water
½ cup Mint Simple Syrup (page 16)
1 (750 milliliter) bottle of brut-style Prosecco
1 lemon, sliced into thin rings

Instructions
Place the ice ring into a punch bowl. Combine the first 4 ingredients. Give them a gentle stir. Pour in the Prosecco. Garnish with lemon slices. Ladle into punch cups and serve.

SPARKLING SIDECAR PUNCH

(Serves 10)

This is another classic cocktail that translates well into a larger format drink for a crowd—and is even more delicious with the addition of a brut-style Prosecco. While you can make most of the punch ahead of time, remember not to add the Prosecco until just before your guests arrive. That way, the bubbles will stay bubbly for a while after they arrive.

Ingredients
1 ice ring (page 19)
1 cup brandy
¼ cup triple sec
¾ cup freshly squeezed lemon juice
½ cup Simple Syrup (page 16)
1 (750 milliliter) bottle of brut-style Prosecco
1 lemon, sliced into thin rings

Instructions
Place the ice ring into a punch bowl. Combine the first 4 ingredients. Give them a gentle stir. Pour in the Prosecco. Garnish with the lemon slices. Ladle into punch cups and serve.

GREYHOUND PUNCH

(Serves 12 to 14)

Modern versions of the Greyhound more often than not use vodka—a blank slate for the puckery citrus of the grapefruit juice. However, if you're a gin lover (like me!), feel free to sub in a citrusy-style gin.

Ingredients
1 ice ring (page 19)
1 cup vodka
2 cups grapefruit juice
½ cup Honey-Basil Syrup (page 17)
1 (750 milliliter) bottle of extra dry-style Prosecco
1 grapefruit, sliced into rings and then cut into half-moons

Instructions
Place the ice ring into a punch bowl. Combine the first 3 ingredients. Give them a gentle stir. Pour in the Prosecco. Garnish with grapefruit slices. Ladle into punch cups and serve.

BARDSTOWN PUNCH

(Serves 20 to 24)

Be it in Scotland, Ireland, the United States, Canada, or
Japan, tea (iced or hot) spiked with whiskey is enjoyed, and
it is a cross-cultural urge for good reason. It's delicious.
This recipe is a nod to Kentucky, a place that some of
the great American whiskies have long called home, and
where the tradition of sweet tea is a summertime given.

Ingredients
1 ice ring (page 19)
1 ½ cups bourbon
4 cups unsweetened peach tea
½ cup freshly squeezed lemon juice
¾ cup Honey Syrup (page 17)
1 (750 milliliter) bottle of extra dry-style Prosecco
1–2 peaches, cut into thin slices

Instructions
Place the ice ring into a punch bowl. Combine the first
4 ingredients. Give them a gentle stir. Pour in the Prosecco.
Garnish with the peach slices. Ladle into punch cups and serve.

INDEX

143

CREDITS

Amy Zavatto would like to thank:
Editor Hazel Eriksson, for her amazingly good humor,
kindness, and patience. You made what potentially
could have been a really tough process at a really
tough time in my life a joy from start to finish—thank
you, lady. I owe you some seriously good Prosecco.

Alan Tardi, the US Ambassador to Conegliano Valdobbiadene,
for sharing his knowledge, allowing me to feel like I was smack
in the middle of a hilly vineyard, and making me love Prosecco
even more than I did. And Stefanie Schwalb and the Gregory
White team in New York City for their invaluable help, resources,
and generosity. To you all, I raise my glass!

Linda Zavatto and Laura Zavatto—the kind of kick-ass
sisters you could only dream up, but they're really mine.
Pearls, both of you.

Dan Marotta—for being my best critic, loyal taster of
experiments (some better than others), best friend, and the
sparkle in all of my days. Love you, always.

Ruby Taylor would like to thank:
Total babes Lucy and Eddie, and the
dream team in LG1.